ECONOMICS OF ENTERTAINMENT

ECONOMICS OF THE SUPER BOWL

Lizann Flatt

Crabtree Publishing Company
www.crabtreebooks.com

Author: Lizann Flatt
Editor-in-chief: Lionel Bender
Editors: Simon Adams, Rachel Eagen
Proofreaders: Laura Booth, Wendy Scavuzzo
Project coordinator: Kathy Middleton
Design and photo research: Ben White
Cover design: Margaret Amy Salter
Production: Kim Richardson
Print and production coordinator:
    Margaret Amy Salter
Prepress technician: Margaret Amy Salter
Graphics: Stefan Chabluk

Consultant: Laura Ebert, Ph.D., Lecturer in
Economics at the State University of New
York at New Paltz, N.Y.

This book was produced for
Crabtree Publishing Company by
Bender Richardson White.

Photographs and reproductions:
Dreamstime.com: 1 bottom middle (Lawrence Weslowski Jr), 4
middle left (Wisconsinart), 10–11 (Wisconsinart), 16–17 bottom
(Lawrence Weslowski Jr), 18–19 (Sean Pavone), 20–21 top (Kenneth
D Durden), 20–21 bottom (Wisconsinart), 24–25 (Ragarwal123), 25
top left (Jerry Coli), 27 top (Lawrence Weslowski Jr). Getty Images:
6–7 (The Washington Post), 11 middle (Focus on Sport), 12–13, 22–
23 (Boston Globe), 26–27 bottom (Boston Globe), 32–33, 33 middle
(fstop123), 34–35 (Jeff Kravitz/FilmMagic), 36–37, 38–39 (Erika
Goldring) , 40–41 (Sports Illustrated), 41 top left (MCT), 42–43
(Toronto Star). Shutterstock.com: cover-bottom left inset (aceshot1),
cover-top right and bottom right insets (Anthony Correia), cover-
top left inset (Ken Durden), cover-center (Richard Paul Kane),
banners (aceshot1), icons (RTimages, Mike Flippo, Trinacria Photo,
Nicholas Piccillo, Kletr), 4–5 (Christopher Penler), 8–9 (Richard
Paul Kane), 14–15 (Richard Paul Kane), 16–17 top (aceshot1), 28–29
(Richard Paul Kane), 29 bottom (Richard Paul Kane), 30–31
(Richard Paul Kane), 42 bottom (Padmayogini).
AOL, Apple, iPad, Android, Coca Cola, AFL, NFL, Super Bowl,
Fox, ESPN, NBC, CBS, Verizon, AT&T, Levi Strauss, MainGate, Inc.
and other manufacturers and brands are registered trademarks
and/or are protected by copyright. They are usually given with a
™, ®, or © symbol.

Library and Archives Canada Cataloguing in Publication

Flatt, Lizann, author
    The economics of the Super Bowl / Lizann Flatt.

(Economics of entertainment)
Includes index.
Issued in print and electronic formats.
ISBN 978-0-7787-7972-8 (bound).--ISBN 978-0-7787-7977-3 (pbk.).--
ISBN 978-1-4271-7871-8 (pdf).--ISBN 978-1-4271-7986-9 (html)

    1. Super Bowl--Economic aspects--Juvenile literature. I. Title.

GV956.2.S8F53 2014   j796.332'648   C2013-907577-1
                                              C2013-907578-X

Library of Congress Cataloging-in-Publication Data

Flatt, Lizann.
 The economics of the Super Bowl / Lizann Flatt.
    pages cm. -- (Economics of entertainment)
 Includes index.
 ISBN 978-0-7787-7972-8 (reinforced library binding) -- ISBN
978-0-7787-7977-3 (pbk.) -- ISBN 978-1-4271-7871-8 (electronic
pdf) -- ISBN 978-1-4271-7986-9 (electronic html)
 1. Super Bowl--Economic aspects. 2. Sports--United States--
Finance. I. Title.

GV956.2.S8F53 2014
796.332'648--dc23

                              2013043401

Crabtree Publishing Company

www.crabtreebooks.com   1-800-387-7650

Printed in Canada/022014/MA20131220

Published in Canada
Crabtree Publishing
616 Welland Ave.
St. Catharines, ON
L2M 5V6

Published in the United States
Crabtree Publishing
PMB 59051
350 Fifth Avenue, 59th Floor
New York, New York 10118

Published in the United Kingdom
Crabtree Publishing
Maritime House
Basin Road North, Hove
BN41 1WR

Published in Australia
Crabtree Publishing
3 Charles Street
Coburg North
VIC, 3058

CONTENTS

WHAT IS THE SUPER BOWL?

Two football teams battle on a field. The winner of this game, the Super Bowl, will claim the title as the year's best team in the National Football League (NFL). Tens of thousands of fans cheer from the stands. Millions more watch on television, computers, and other devices. It's an event that costs—and makes—millions of dollars. Why all the hype?

Tickets to be in the stadium at Super Bowl XLV cost $800 each. People are willing to pay a high price to be at this one-of-a-kind event.

A stadium hosting a Super Bowl game is packed with fans. Only the first Super Bowl in January 1967 failed to sell out all seats.

SUPER SPECTACLE

The single game to determine the year's winning NFL team makes the Super Bowl exciting. With one Super Bowl a year, you don't want to miss the game. The game is held on a Sunday in January or February in a different city each year. That city attracts many thousands of football fans who come to the game. The city hopes these people will spend money on hotels, restaurants, and other entertainment while they're in town.

The NFL is a **producer** because it makes the Super Bowl. It **distributes** the Super Bowl by charging money for others to watch it through ticket sales and TV or Internet broadcasts. The NFL makes a **profit** from producing the Super Bowl. When businesses produce things to sell and make money, we call this **capitalism**.

FOOTBALL FOUNDER VINCE LOMBARDI

The trophy hoisted by the winning team is called the Vince Lombardi Trophy. Lombardi was the coach of the Green Bay Packers, leading them to victory in the first two Super Bowls. He died of cancer in 1970. That same year, the Super Bowl trophy was named in his honor.

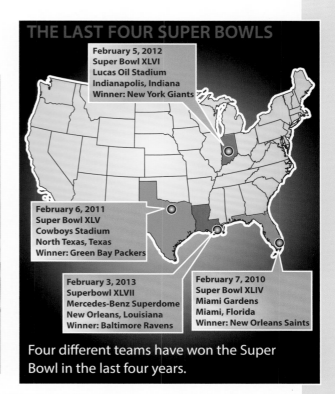

THE LAST FOUR SUPER BOWLS

February 5, 2012
Super Bowl XLVI
Lucas Oil Stadium
Indianapolis, Indiana
Winner: New York Giants

February 6, 2011
Super Bowl XLV
Cowboys Stadium
North Texas, Texas
Winner: Green Bay Packers

February 3, 2013
Superbowl XLVII
Mercedes-Benz Superdome
New Orleans, Louisiana
Winner: Baltimore Ravens

February 7, 2010
Super Bowl XLIV
Miami Gardens
Miami, Florida
Winner: New Orleans Saints

Four different teams have won the Super Bowl in the last four years.

WHAT IS ECONOMICS?

ECONOMICS

Economics is the study of how goods (such as shirts or footballs), services (such as a dental checkup), and resources (such as water or oil) get from the people that make or provide them (the producers) to the people who use them (the consumers), like you. The economic system used in the United States is called a **market economy**. In this system, everyone has the freedom to choose what goods, services, and resources they consume.

To put this another way, when you use goods, services, or resources, you are a **consumer**. You consume or use things you need such as food, clothing, and a place to live. You will pay for these things because you need them. But what about the things you don't need, such as a ticket to a football game? You might want a ticket. But if you buy one, that means you won't be able to buy something else with that money. Of course, you can decide to consume things you want but don't necessarily need. Economics often involves making choices.

BUDGETS

No person, business, organization, or government has an unlimited supply of money, so everyone has to decide how much of their money goes toward the things they need and the things they want. A detailed plan that manages money received, expenses, and available spending money is called a **budget**. When you make money, that's called **income**. When you spend money, that's known as an **expense**. Many people make an income working in the sports **industry**. When you decide to budget some of your allowance for game tickets or buy a football to practice with your friends, you are acting as a consumer and supporting the sports industry.

WHAT DO YOU THINK?

There are a limited number of seats in a football stadium, so there is a limited supply of tickets. If lots of people want to buy tickets, would you expect the price of a ticket to be low or high in price? What would a demand greater than the number of tickets available do to the price? A price that changes based on demand is called elastic.

Money left over after you have paid all your bills and expenses is known as disposable income. You can spend it on a Pro-football Hall of Famer Jersey.

SCARCITY

The quantity of a good or service available is called the **supply**. The **demand** is how much of that good or service people are willing and able to buy. There's only one Super Bowl a year, which means there's a limited supply of Super Bowls. When there is a low supply of something relative to demand, called an excess demand, people are willing to pay more. Businesses can ask for more money for a product where the supply is scarce because lots of people want it and they're willing to pay more to get it. This in turn means more profit for the business. This is why prices are flexible.

Supply and demand will always affect price in a market economy. It works the other way, too. If there's a high supply of a good relative to demand, called excess supply, the price will fall.

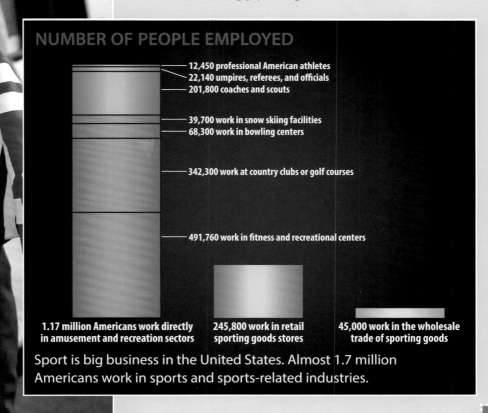

NUMBER OF PEOPLE EMPLOYED

- 12,450 professional American athletes
- 22,140 umpires, referees, and officials
- 201,800 coaches and scouts
- 39,700 work in snow skiing facilities
- 68,300 work in bowling centers
- 342,300 work at country clubs or golf courses
- 491,760 work in fitness and recreational centers

1.17 million Americans work directly in amusement and recreation sectors

245,800 work in retail sporting goods stores

45,000 work in the wholesale trade of sporting goods

Sport is big business in the United States. Almost 1.7 million Americans work in sports and sports-related industries.

1 SUPERNOMICS

Just think of all the money that is exchanged at a football game. Every person bought a ticket, and maybe souvenirs, too. Did they drive a car to get to the game, or travel by train or bus? Consumers create demand for goods and services, which boosts the amount of money generated by those goods and services.

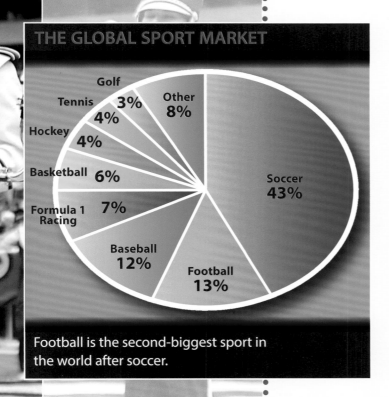

The following text block appears over the photo:

Members of the Temple University marching band perform on the field prior to a game on September 17, 2011, at Lincoln Financial Field in Philadelphia, Pennsylvania.

THE GLOBAL SPORT MARKET

Golf 3%
Tennis 4%
Hockey 4%
Basketball 6%
Formula 1 Racing 7%
Baseball 12%
Football 13%
Other 8%
Soccer 43%

Football is the second-biggest sport in the world after soccer.

MACRO AND MICRO MEASUREMENT

When we combine all of society's demand from individual households, businesses, government, and other countries who want our goods, we call it **aggregate demand**. The study of aggregate demand combined with the study of the total supply of goods and services, called aggregate supply, is the focus of **macroeconomics**. When you look at demand and supply at an individual level, such as how a family budgets its money, that's called **microeconomics**. Macro- and microeconomics work together. The state of the country's economy affects the availability of jobs and the **wages** for those jobs in the country. That in turn affects how much money people can spend on things such as tickets to a game.

GENERATING DEMAND

The **market** for football is one of the biggest sports markets in the world. A lot of people pay to consume it by watching the game and buying game **merchandise**. In fact, the professional football industry, including the Super Bowl, is so huge it generates its own demand. That means city governments want to host the Super Bowl to attract people to their city. Many companies want to be a part of the Super Bowl so they can promote their goods and services. So many people watch the game that it makes even more people watch the game so they, too, know what everyone is talking about.

ADDING TO THE AUDIENCE

In 1920, the American Professional Football League formed but changed its name in 1922 to the National Football League. In the early days, people felt professional football was not as good as college football. People criticized the idea that athletes would play football for money. Many early professional players had day jobs.

The invention of television created a potential national audience for professional football. Before television, most people were more interested in their local high school or college football team. Before 1956, an NFL TV blackout policy meant that people in the home-team city had to buy tickets to watch the game at the stadium while the rest of the country watched the game on television. The NFL felt this policy protected the home team's gate **receipt** income while helping to increase the popularity of the game everywhere else.

In 1960, the American Football League formed with its own TV contract to broadcast games. By 1966, the AFL (American Football League) and NFL had agreed to merge. Keeping the name NFL, the league divided itself into two regions, called conferences: the American Football Conference and the National Football Conference. The first Super Bowl, a championship game between the two conferences, was played in 1967. The name Super Bowl was first used in 1969 and each annual game thereafter was given a Roman numeral.

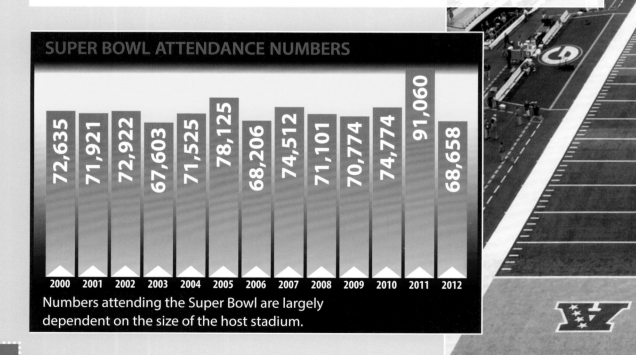

SUPER BOWL ATTENDANCE NUMBERS

2000	2001	2002	2003	2004	2005	2006	2007	2008	2009	2010	2011	2012
72,635	71,921	72,922	67,603	71,525	78,125	68,206	74,512	71,101	70,774	74,774	91,060	68,658

Numbers attending the Super Bowl are largely dependent on the size of the host stadium.

Cowboys Stadium in Dallas, Texas, hosted Super Bowl XLV between the Pittsburgh Steelers and the Green Bay Packers on February 6, 2011. They hoped to beat the Super Bowl attendance record by adding extra seats. But, due to safety issues, they couldn't use the seats. The ticket holders were reseated elsewhere, or given a refund of three times the price they paid for their tickets.

The first Super Bowl was held on January 15, 1967. The Green Bay Packers defeated the Kansas City Chiefs at the Memorial Coliseum in Los Angeles, California.

2 WHO MAKES MONEY?

The Super Bowl is one game on one day, but it takes a lot of time, hard work, and money to put on a Super Bowl. Teams work and play games all season, television networks plan and broadcast stories to generate interest in the game, and cities compete for the right to host the big game, and prepare for the big day. All of them spend lots of money. Why? Because all of them expect to make huge profits.

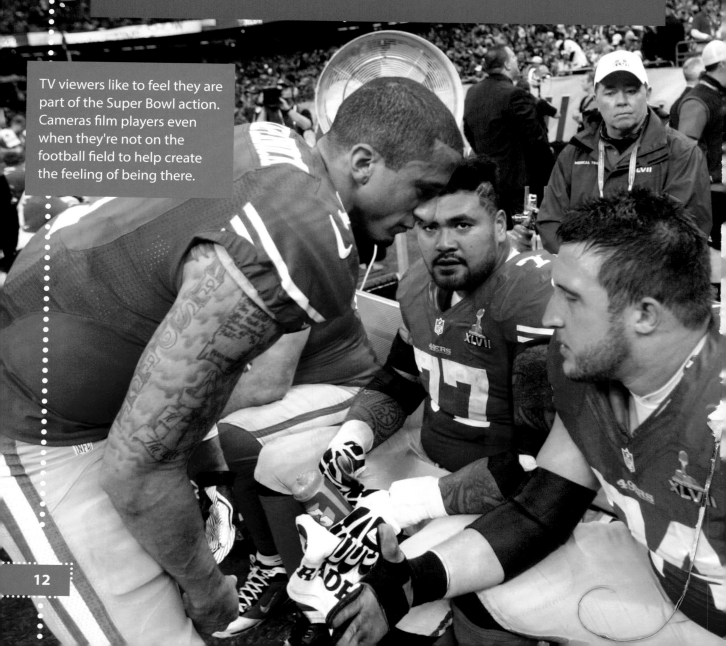

TV viewers like to feel they are part of the Super Bowl action. Cameras film players even when they're not on the football field to help create the feeling of being there.

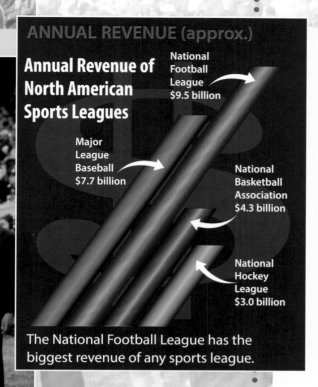

ANNUAL REVENUE (approx.)

Annual Revenue of North American Sports Leagues

National Football League
$9.5 billion

Major League Baseball
$7.7 billion

National Basketball Association
$4.3 billion

National Hockey League
$3.0 billion

The National Football League has the biggest revenue of any sports league.

WHAT DO YOU THINK?

The company A.C. Nielsen provides statistics on what people watch on television. In 2013, Super Bowl XLVII reached an estimated audience of 164.1 million viewers. That made it the most watched broadcast in American history. How do you think delivering the game to all those viewers influences the price the NFL can ask a TV network for the right to show the game?

SUPER BRAND

Have you ever bought a hat or maybe a T-shirt with the Super Bowl logo on it? That Super Bowl logo helps identify things that are official Super Bowl merchandise. The logo is part of a **brand** the NFL has created around itself and the Super Bowl. A brand creates revenue when businesses and consumers purchase things because of their relationship to that brand.

Maybe you wouldn't pay $20 for a T-shirt. But if it had the Super Bowl logo on it, you might buy it to show you had been there. Branding influences you to buy an item you might not have bought otherwise. That's the value of a strong brand, and one reason why NFL revenue was more than $9 billion in 2013.

SUPER SALES

Having a strong brand gives the NFL other **revenue streams** in addition to merchandise sales. The TV networks pay to broadcast the Super Bowl to attract viewers and advertisers to their network. Cities spend money to host a Super Bowl to attract consumers to their city as millions of people talk about the game. Companies buy space to put their own logos up in the stadium where they can be seen by millions. Companies **sponsor** the coin toss or the halftime show so their name is mentioned in connection with the Super Bowl. NFL football teams work hard all season to make it to the Super Bowl for team satisfaction and to increase their fan base.

SOURCES OF INCOME

Football teams make money from game ticket sales, concession sales of food, drinks, and souvenirs; merchandise **license** fees (money from selling other companies the right to make official NFL team merchandise), and TV rights. The home team keeps profits from food and drink sales and parking at their home stadium. The amount of profit varies depending on the size of the stadium and on the **lease** contract (a rental agreement) with the stadium. For example, the Atlanta Falcons earned $500,000 from one game, whereas the New England Patriots have received more than $2 million.

The NFL collects the ticket sales revenue from all the NFL teams' games, then distributes 60 percent of the money to home teams and 40 percent to visiting teams. In 2012, the league distributed $17 million in ticket sales. The NFL

WHAT DO YOU THINK?

After a successful college football career that won him the Heisman Trophy, Tim Tebow has a large fan following. But, in the NFL, he has struggled to play quarterback well. Can you use the concept of demand to explain one possible reason a team might want to sign him? Could you argue that he brings with him **intangible** benefits?

VALUE OF TOP TEN MOST VALUABLE NFL TEAMS

1. Dallas Cowboys ············· $2,100,000,000
2. New England Patriots ········· $1,635,000,000
3. Washington Redskins ········· $1,600,000,000
4. New York Giants ·········· $1,468,000,000
5. Houston Texans ········· $1,305,000,000
6. New York Jets ··········· $1,284,000,000
7. Philadelphia Eagles ···· $1,260,000,000
8. Chicago Bears ········ $1,190,000,000
9. San Francisco 49ers · $1,175,000,000
10. Green Bay Packers ·· $1,161,000,000

In 2012, the top ten most valuable NFL teams were each worth more than $1 billion. Figures are rounded to millions.

also divides the money received from TV broadcast deals (at least $6 billion a year) and merchandise licensing, then shares it equally between all the teams in the league.

DO PLAYOFFS PAY?

The NFL gives the teams in the playoffs a payment for each game to help cover travel and other expenses, and also to pay their players during the playoffs (player contracts only cover the regular season). But if a team isn't doing much more than covering its expenses, why would it bother being in the playoffs? That's because of the intangible benefits of being in the Super Bowl, such as more fans for the team.

Where do NFL teams find new players? They're often chosen, or drafted, from college football teams such as the Buffalo Bulls and Temple Owls, shown here.

SUPER BOWL AUDIENCE

MANY WAYS TO WATCH

Do you want to watch the Super Bowl live at the stadium? You're not alone. In 2012, at Super Bowl XLVI in Indianapolis, Indiana, 68,658 people watched at the stadium. Because a stadium holds a limited number of spectators, the NFL looks for other ways to increase its audience and therefore increase its revenue.

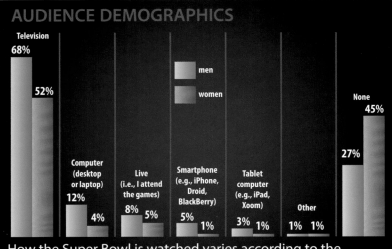

AUDIENCE DEMOGRAPHICS

- Television: men 68%, women 52%
- Computer (desktop or laptop): men 12%, women 4%
- Live (i.e., I attend the games): men 8%, women 5%
- Smartphone (e.g., iPhone, Droid, BlackBerry): men 5%, women 1%
- Tablet computer (e.g., iPad, Xoom): men 3%, women 1%
- Other: men 1%, women 1%
- None: men 27%, women 45%

Legend: men, women

How the Super Bowl is watched varies according to the gender of the viewer.

The Bank of America Stadium in Charlotte, North Carolina, is packed with fans even during a regular season game, as in this game between the Washington Redskins and the Carolina Panthers in January 2010.

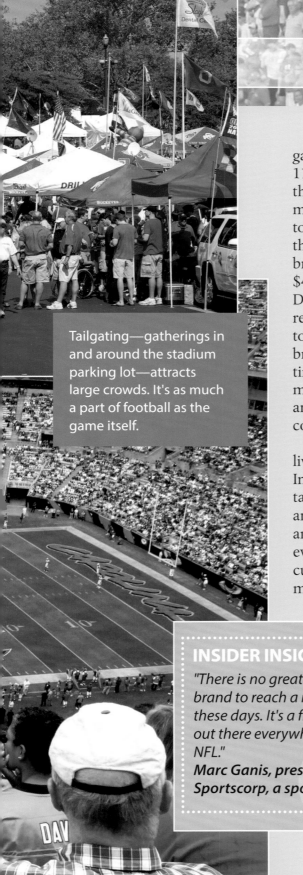

Tailgating—gatherings in and around the stadium parking lot—attracts large crowds. It's as much a part of football as the game itself.

Television allows millions of people to see the game. That Super Bowl in Indianapolis? Another 111,346,000 viewers saw it on TV. Even though those viewers don't pay for tickets, the NFL still makes money on those viewers. It sells its audience to TV companies for additional revenue. In 2011, the revenue deal for NBC, Fox, CBS, and ESPN to broadcast NFL football games through to 2019 is $42 billion. Revenue from satellite TV provider DirecTV is an additional $1 billion until the deal is renegotiated in 2014. TV broadcasters are willing to pay so much money to the NFL because the broadcasters turn around and sell TV commercial time to other businesses. The network provides millions of Super Bowl viewers to the businesses and charges them enough money for a 30-second commercial spot so that the network makes a profit.

Besides television, there are people watching live-streaming video on their computers over the Internet. Owners of Verizon mobile phones and tablets can watch live-stream games in their local areas on a special NFL app. That brings the NFL another $1 billion over four years. This gives the NFL even more viewers and fans, and Verizon gets more customers who will pay for the service to use its mobile data network.

INSIDER INSIGHT

"There is no greater way for a brand to reach a mass audience these days. It's a fragmented world out there everywhere else but the NFL."
Marc Ganis, president of Sportscorp, a sports consultancy

WHO IS WATCHING?

Who are these fans? Super Bowl viewers are more likely to be from higher income homes. Nielsen found that 45 percent of all households watched Super Bowl XLVI. This vast audience is a valuable asset for the NFL because it can sell access to that audience to TV broadcasters.

THE BID FOR THE SUPER BOWL

REASONS TO COMPETE

Would you want the world's eyes on your city so you could let the world know why your city is such a great place? Want to increase your city's revenue by attracting thousands of visitors? This is why cities compete to host a Super Bowl. The NFL awards a Super Bowl to a host city four years in advance. The 32 NFL team owners cast a vote after reviewing **bids** from potential host cities. This competitive process lets the NFL choose the best cities.

A host city needs to provide many resources such as a stadium that seats more than 70,000 people, at least 24,500 hotel rooms within an hour of the stadium, and an extra 2 million square feet (0.9 million square meters) of event space for other attractions held for fans during the Super Bowl. These include Super Bowl Boulevard (an area for games, food, and free concerts) and the NFL Experience (interactive displays of football skills and special events). In addition, a host city needs to have an NFL team in the city or region. Not every city can provide this, so the market for hosting a Super Bowl can be called **oligopolistic**—only a limited number of cities can participate.

Cities create bids or written proposals to highlight the resources their city has to offer the NFL. It's a very competitive process. Indianapolis chose 32 kids in the eighth grade and sent each, with a chaperone, to hand-deliver a proposal to each of the 32 NFL team owners. Indianapolis won the bid and hosted Super Bowl XLVI.

EXTERNALITIES

The decision to host the Super Bowl affects other unrelated businesses. These are called **externalities**. Cities hope to take advantage of positive externalities by hosting a Super Bowl. Spectators will stay at area hotels, eat at restaurants, and shop for souvenirs. Airlines and gas stations see increased business. Individuals rent their homes or allow people to park on their property for added income. Before a Super Bowl, host cities improve their roads and other infrastructure. This benefits not only the people who fix the roads, but also those people who use the newer roads long after the game is over.

INSIDER INSIGHT

"It is an event that provides weeks of unprecedented global media coverage for a community, and that community is talked about for the whole year leading up to the game, and, of course, there is no denying the hundreds of millions of dollars in economic impact generated for these host communities."
Greg Bensel, vice president of New Orleans Saints

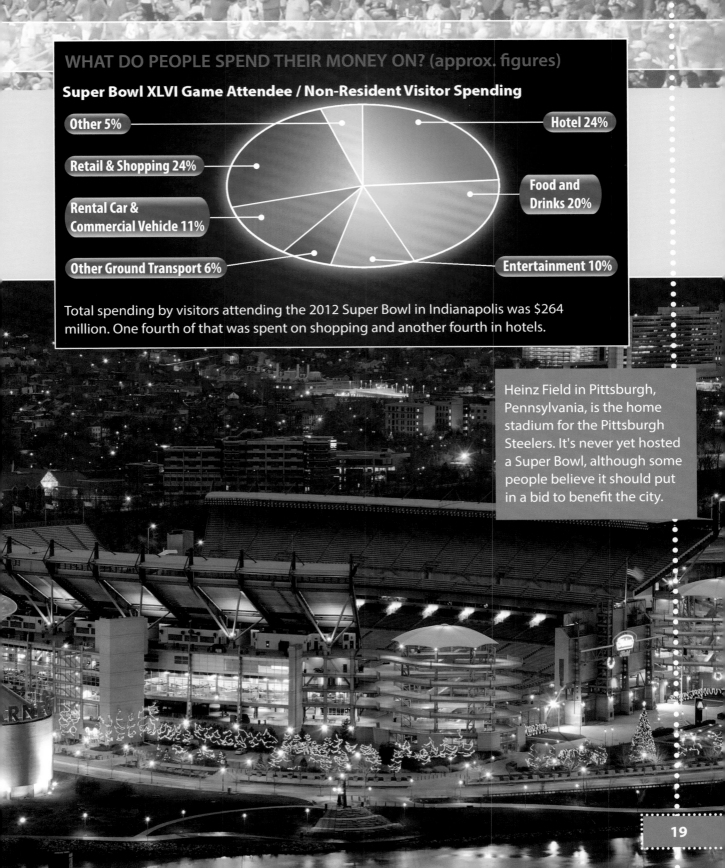

WHAT DO PEOPLE SPEND THEIR MONEY ON? (approx. figures)

Super Bowl XLVI Game Attendee / Non-Resident Visitor Spending

Other 5%

Retail & Shopping 24%

Rental Car & Commercial Vehicle 11%

Other Ground Transport 6%

Hotel 24%

Food and Drinks 20%

Entertainment 10%

Total spending by visitors attending the 2012 Super Bowl in Indianapolis was $264 million. One fourth of that was spent on shopping and another fourth in hotels.

Heinz Field in Pittsburgh, Pennsylvania, is the home stadium for the Pittsburgh Steelers. It's never yet hosted a Super Bowl, although some people believe it should put in a bid to benefit the city.

THE STADIUM

STADIUM ASSETS

A football stadium generates revenue through the sale of food, drinks, and souvenirs, but bigger money is made selling other stadium **assets**. Do you want to watch the game in comfort? Luxury suites at MetLife Stadium have a private road to the **VIP** parking, a private entrance, special washrooms, several flat-panel screens, and a bar. Fans with tickets for club seats are entitled to wider cushioned seats along with special parking and access to exclusive lounges. Revenue from club seats and luxury suites for the Cowboys, Washington Redskins, and New York Giants gives each team about $75 million a year.

Teams also sell a more intangible item called personal seat licenses, or PSLs. This is a payment that guarantees you can purchase tickets to a specific seat for a public event at the stadium. The San Francisco 49ers have set PSL prices for their new stadium ranging from $20,000 to $80,000 a seat.

In Dallas, Texas, the Cowboys' venue was called simply Cowboys Stadium when it first opened in 2009. In 2013, a deal for $500 million over 25 years bought AT&T the right to have the venue renamed the AT&T Stadium.

Luxury suites are private rooms that companies buy so their executives or important clients can watch the game in comfort. The suites have an excellent view of the field and many other expensive perks.

WHAT DO YOU THINK?

Food and drinks at the stadium cost more than you would pay for the same items at your local restaurant. At Super Bowl XLVII in 2013, hot dogs cost as much as $9, nachos $14, bottled water $5, and soda in a souvenir cup $8. Ouch! That hurts the pocket. Can you use the idea of competition to explain why the prices are so high?

How about a stadium's name? That's for sale, too. When a company names a stadium, the company's name is mentioned every time the football game is mentioned. That means you become more aware of that company. In 2013, the San Francisco 49ers finalized a $220 million deal with Levi Strauss & Co for naming rights to their stadium in Santa Clara, California. The stadium will be called Levi Stadium, giving the 49ers $11 million a year for 20 years. In exchange, Levis will have signs with its name on them around the stadium and on the end-zone scoreboards, the large restaurant inside will be named Club 501 for its 501 jeans, and cheerleaders and the 49ers' mascot will wear Levis clothes.

SHINY NEW STADIUMS

Teams want to add value to the stadium experience. New stadiums have large screens for broadcasting the game to people in the upper decks. They also have more washroom facilities and plenty of space for businesses to sell their products to consumers.

THE BIG GAME

The Super Bowl is more than just a football game. Additional attractions give **value-added** experiences to the fans who attend the game. The game's own logo, made of Roman numerals, is constructed as a large physical attraction that fans can visit. The Vince Lombardi Trophy is put on display for visitors to see. Each city puts on the events surrounding the game, which can include the NFL Experience, Super Bowl Boulevard, and the NFL Tailgate Party.

COST OF SUPER BOWL TICKETS

2012 $1,200 to $600 Lucas Oil Stadium, Indianapolis, Indiana

2011 $1,200 to $600 Cowboys Stadium, Arlington, Texas

2010 $1,000 to $500 Sun Life Stadium, Miami, Florida

2009 $1,000 to $500 Raymond James Stadium, Tampa, Florida

2008 $900, $700 University of Phoenix Stadium, Glendale, Arizona

2007 $700, $600 Dolphin Stadium, Miami, Florida

From 2003 to 2012 there was a range of ticket prices

2006 $700, $600 Ford Field, Detroit, Michigan

2005 $600, $500 ALLTEL Stadium, Jacksonville, Florida

2004 $600, $500, $600 Reliant Stadium, Houston, Texas

2003 $500, $400 Qualcomm Stadium, San Diego, California

2002 $400 Superdome, New Orleans, Louisiana

2001 $325 Raymond James Stadium, Tampa, Florida

2000 $325 Georgia Dome, Atlanta, Georgia

The cost of Super Bowl tickets rose from $325 in 2000 to $1,200 in 2012.

Tickets to Super Bowl games can resell for much higher than their face value. But be sure your ticket is real. Several security features, such as holograms, glossy finishes, and laser cutouts, are built into authentic tickets.

BASIC ECONOMICS

Inflation is a measure of the rate at which the prices for goods and services rise in a year. As inflation rises, a dollar has less value because it buys less than it did before because goods and services cost more.

WHAT DO YOU THINK?

Some people resell their tickets for more money than they paid for them. The NFL makes ticket reselling possible through the Ticket Exchange. This official marketplace helps ensure that people don't buy fake tickets. Given what you know about ticket availability, why might someone buy a ticket for more than the face value? What benefit would the NFL see in helping fans to resell tickets?

DO YOU HAVE A TICKET?

Super Bowl tickets are controlled by the NFL. It gives 17.5 percent of tickets to the AFC Championship team and 17.5 percent to the NFC champions. Another 5 percent is given to the host city's football team. Then 35.8 percent is divided between all the other teams in the NFL, and the last 24.2 percent goes to the NFL itself. Tickets are given to sponsors, celebrities, former football legends, and season ticket holders in a random draw.

The only way for the general public to get Super Bowl tickets is through the NFL's random draw or through a ticket reseller. For the draw, people apply by mail to the NFL between February and June each year. If your name is one of the approximately 1,000 drawn, you'll be told in October or November. Then you can buy two tickets.

MORE THAN A GAME

To give a value-added experience to the Super Bowl, the NFL developed other game-day-related attractions. The NFL Experience is an interactive football theme park that opens several days before the Super Bowl and continues up to and including game day. It includes games, football clinics for kids, autograph sessions with players, and merchandise for sale. Tickets to the 2013 Experience in New Orleans, Louisiana, cost $25 for adults and $20 for children. Indianapolis, Indiana, was the first to create the Super Bowl Village in 2012 to bring people downtown for concerts, games, and free entertainment. In 2013, that idea was renamed Super Bowl Boulevard and used in New Orleans.

SPONSORSHIP

Why is almost everything at the Super Bowl associated with a company? The answer is sponsorship. The Super Bowl has such a large viewership that lots of other companies want to be associated with it. Becoming the official sponsor of anything related to the game pays off for companies in the form of better brand recognition. Companies know that if you're aware of a brand, you're likely to buy that brand.

Only official marketing partners are allowed to use the name Super Bowl. There are 22 such companies that pay the NFL about $100 million a year for the right to use the game's name and logo in their ads. Papa John's became the official pizza of the Super Bowl in 2010.

TRICKS OF THE TRADE

While the NFL is not involved in betting and gambling, in 2011, $1.34 billion, or 41 percent of all sports-related betting, was related to football. The gambling industry benefits from football, and football benefits from the increased interest from gamblers.

FANTASY SPORTS (approximate figures)

Percentage of Fantasy Sports Players Compared to Population of Age 12+ in the United States (33+ Million Players) and Canada (3+ Million Players)

	U.S.	Canada
Total	13%	12%
Adults	13%	12%
Teens	13%	11%
Male	19%	20%
Female	8%	5%
College Education	18%	22%
No College Education	10%	11%
Household Income $50K+	16%	15%
Household Income <$50K	10%	10%

On average, fantasy sports players spend $111 on league-related costs, single-player challenge games, and league related materials over a 12-month period

	Per Player	U.S. Market Share
League Fees	$52	$1.71 Billion
Transaction Fees	$8	$262 Million
Website Hosting Fees	$9	$290 Million
Website Prize Fees	$7	$230 Million
Information Materials	$20	$656 Million
Challenge Games	$15	$492 Million

In 2013, more than 33 million people played fantasy sports in the United States and another 3 million in Canada.

In New York's Times Square, advertisers who sponsor the game use the Super Bowl logo to promote themselves while promoting the Super Bowl at the same time.

For the Super Bowl in Indianapolis, Roman numerals 30 feet (9 m) long by 82 feet (25 m) high weighing 96 tons (87 tonnes) were lit and featured video images and music.

Game day is its biggest sales day of the year. Pepsi, the official league soda, saw its brand awareness rise by 8 percent while Coca-Cola's has declined 15 percent.

FANTASY FOOTBALL

In Fantasy Football, people make up fantasy teams using real football statistics based on how players do in real NFL games. The Fantasy Sports Trade Association says about 25.1 million people play fantasy football, spending $2.54 billion. Stadiums now try to capture revenue from this audience by creating special fantasy sports lounges with high definition (HD) TVs and Internet access to allow players to make changes to their fantasy teams. This increased interest in the fantasy game is an **indirect benefit** to the NFL because it increases overall fan interest in real teams.

BIDDING

Have you worn a hat sporting your favorite football team's logo? Played the EA Sports' football video game? Then you've seen merchandising in action. In 1963, NFL Properties was created as a **subsidiary** company to the NFL. It looks after the licensing and merchandising for the NFL.

The Super Bowl, individual teams, and the NFL each have a logo that's put on merchandise.

TRICKS OF THE TRADE

Super Bowl team winning shirts and hats are out as soon as the final whistle blows, because manufacturers preprint them for both teams. So what happens to all that apparel created for the losing team? It used to just be destroyed, but that's a waste of resources. Now the major sports leagues and major sports apparel manufacturers donate the misprinted items to World Vision, a charity that gives the merchandise to people living in poverty or in disaster regions all over the world.

How do you show you're a fan? You can buy just about anything with your favorite football team's logo on it. Your action to buy official football merchandise is one way you support the NFL.

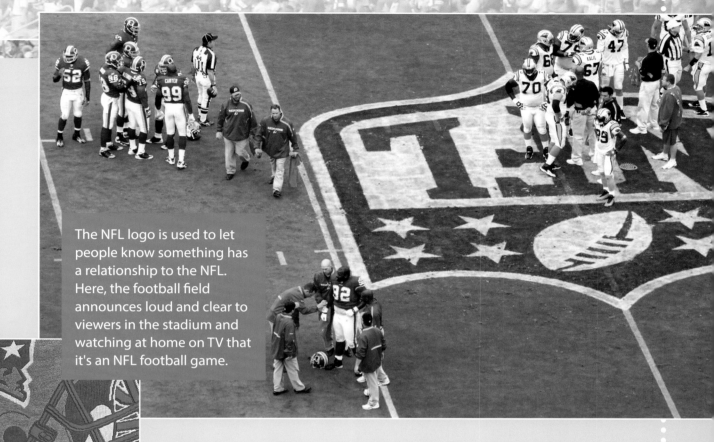

The NFL logo is used to let people know something has a relationship to the NFL. Here, the football field announces loud and clear to viewers in the stadium and watching at home on TV that it's an NFL football game.

But the NFL isn't in the business of making and selling goods and souvenirs, or merchandise, with its logos on them. Instead, it licenses or gives permission for other companies to make and sell these goods in return for a fee. This means that companies pay the NFL for the right to put the Super Bowl and other NFL logos on their merchandise.

BIDDING FOR BUCKS

Companies that want to sell official Super Bowl merchandise send proposals to the NFL in a competitive bidding process. The NFL chooses the companies that best meet their needs and have the best proposal, which can include the best offer for percentage of sales going to the NFL. But the NFL does not choose just one company. It **fragments**, or breaks up, the market for its merchandise to take better advantage of sales from different companies. For the 2014 Super Bowl, MainGate, Inc. won the contract to sell merchandise at 40 hotels during the ten-day celebrations leading up to and including Super Bowl Sunday. The company beat 14 other bids to handle these sales for the NFL in exchange for a small cut of each sale. A different company won the contract to sell merchandise inside the stadium on game day.

THE HIDDEN EVENT COSTS

Hosting a Super Bowl brings in a lot of revenue but it costs a lot as well. People have to be paid to work at the stadium, teams have to get there, and the city has to prepare the stadium.

Indianapolis built Lucas Oil Stadium for $720 million to host Super Bowl XLVI. The Indianapolis Colts paid $100 million of that. The state, county, and city all raised money for the project. The county raised **taxes** on things such as food and drink sales, car rentals, hotels, and more while other cities have added a 1 percent tax to all restaurant meal bills to fund their stadiums. For the event itself, the city planned for $4 million for public safety costs. About 1,500 law enforcement officers were employed in the city over the weekend.

A team going to the Super Bowl incurs expenses to get there. It pays transportation costs for the players and coaches. Football players are paid an average annual **salary** of $1.93 million. Coaches' salaries are private but some head coaches are paid up to $7 million a year. Team cheerleaders are paid anywhere from $500 to $700 a season, with sometimes a bit extra for special appearances. The NFL pays referees about $173,000 a year.

Stadiums have to employ people to take tickets, sell food and drinks at concession stands, provide security, clean up after events, run the office, keep washrooms clean and stocked, and so on. More than 500 people work at the stadium on game day.

OTHER OPPORTUNITIES

So is hosting the Super Bowl worth it? That depends on what else the city or the stadium could have been doing that weekend. Would, say, holding a rock concert have brought in more money or cost less? The cost of an alternative not chosen is called the **opportunity cost**.

Some of these college cheerleaders may go on to compete for a spot on an NFL cheerleading squad. Cheerleading is a part-time job in the NFL. Once on the squad, cheerleaders practice a couple of times a week and go to every game.

TOP SALARIES AND TEAMS 2013-2014

Overall payrolls

Seattle Seahawks	$124,900,000
Minnesota Vikings	$122,600,000
Cincinnati Bengals	$119,700,000
Chicago Bears	$119,400,000
Denver Broncos	$119,200,000
Green Bay Packers	$118,000,000
New Orleans Saints	$116,600,000
Kansas City Chiefs	$116,300,000
San Francisco 49ers	$116,200,000
Houston Texans	$115,300,000

10 most highly paid players

Aaron Rodgers	$43,000,000	Green Bay Packers
Drew Brees	$40,000,000	New Orleans Saints
Joe Flacco	$35,900,000	Baltimore Ravens
Tom Brady	$31,300,000	New England Patriots
Tony Romo	$25,800,000	Dallas Cowboys
Calvin Johnson	$25,500,000	Detroit Lions
Dwayne Bowe	$24,500,000	Kansas City Chiefs
Ray Rice	$24,200,000	Baltimore Ravens
Vincent Jackson	$23,200,000	Tampa Bay Buccaneers
Peyton Manning	$18,000,000	Denver Broncos

The top ten teams each year spend fortunes on their players and staff. Individual players can earn more than $43 million for salary plus bonuses a year.

A football team pays several coaches on staff. An NFL team generally has a head coach and 15 assistant coaches. A college team may have about nine assistants.

4 MONEY MATTERS

If you produce something, the money you paid to make it is your cost, or expense. The price you sell something for is your revenue. The difference between the revenue and expense is your profit. Companies use the Super Bowl to market their goods and services, hoping to increase sales revenue that in turn increases their profit.

MONOPOLY MARKET

There is only one U.S. professional football league, with one Super Bowl. The NFL is the entire U.S. professional football market, which makes it a **monopoly**. As long as the demand for consuming professional football holds, the NFL can ask whatever price it wants to increase its profits. Of course, if consumers start to think that it's too expensive to consume professional football, they can turn to college football, substitute another sport, or pursue another interest.

Historically, Super Bowl games have been among the most watched programs on TV. So networks are willing to pay billions of dollars to broadcast the game. But of course they want to make a profit, too. The networks turn around and sell commercial or ad spots to other companies, with a **mark-up** on the price of advertising airtime. The Super Bowl broadcast is profitable for them.

IT'S FOR THE FANS

This quest for profit comes down to you, the football fan. The NFL, the networks, the companies that buy ads—they want to profit from you. What better place to market consumer goods than at an event where millions of consumers are paying attention. If you're a football fan, you're not just a football fan. You have other wants and needs: You eat, play games, listen to music, and you may have a cell phone. All types of companies will try to reach you through your interest in the Super Bowl. It's up to you to decide whether to watch the game.

Dramatic takedowns and plays, feats of athleticism, and the intensity of competition all add to the entertainment value and excitement of football.

TV COMMERCIALS

WHO'S WATCHING?

The TV commercials shown during the Super Bowl are just as much a part of the entertainment as the game itself. People actually look forward to, and watch, the ads. Companies are willing to **invest** more than $3.5 million to buy a 30-second ad. Advertisers are willing to pay this because of the huge audience on game day—including about 50 million homes.

Companies that capitalize on these viewers create new or special ads for their Super Bowl spots. Viewership measurement companies have shown that people actually watch the ads shown during the game. This is the complete opposite of most programs, where people get up and leave the room during commercials.

MASS MESSAGES

Such a huge audience is a massive opportunity for a company to launch a new product and an opportunity for brands to change a product's or company's image. Companies can get their message out to a massive number of people at once.

And after the ads are broadcast during the football game, they appear the next day in newscasts to highlight the favorites, and they show up on YouTube and online news stories and even on the NFL's own website. Each time the popular—or even the not-so-popular—commercials are watched or talked about, the company gets its message or at least its name out there in front of people. Many companies think that exposure to such a huge audience is easily worth the millions they've invested in a Super Bowl ad. The Volkswagen car company estimated they received $100 million in free publicity after its Darth Vader commercial made headlines.

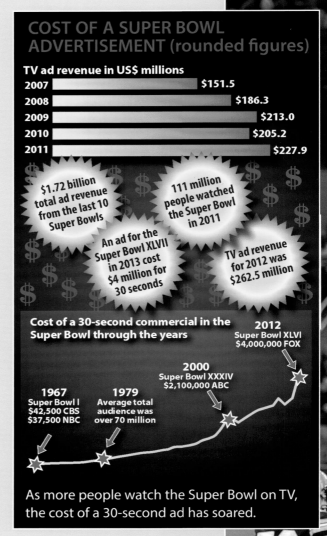

COST OF A SUPER BOWL ADVERTISEMENT (rounded figures)

TV ad revenue in US$ millions

2007	$151.5
2008	$186.3
2009	$213.0
2010	$205.2
2011	$227.9

$1.72 billion total ad revenue from the last 10 Super Bowls

111 million people watched the Super Bowl in 2011

An ad for the Super Bowl XLVII in 2013 cost $4 million for 30 seconds

TV ad revenue for 2012 was $262.5 million

Cost of a 30-second commercial in the Super Bowl through the years

1967 Super Bowl I $42,500 CBS $37,500 NBC

1979 Average total audience was over 70 million

2000 Super Bowl XXXIV $2,100,000 ABC

2012 Super Bowl XLVI $4,000,000 FOX

As more people watch the Super Bowl on TV, the cost of a 30-second ad has soared.

Football fans who watch the game at home are the target audience for about 55 commercials per game.

Television cameras are everywhere on game day, filming from all angles.

THE HALFTIME SHOW

MASS EXPOSURE

In the middle of the Super Bowl, the Halftime Show entertains the crowd. In the early days, it was a marching band but now it's grown to a huge rock concert. But believe it or not, the performers don't get paid to perform. Michael Jackson, U2, Madonna, the Black Eyed Peas, and Beyoncé were not paid. Why did they perform for free? The benefit to the halftime performer is exposure to potential fans.

MINI CONCERT

The halftime show is a rock concert. The NFL pays $600,000 toward the costs of production such as the backup singers, dancers, and musicians. But shows often cost several million dollars and more. The performer may have a sponsor to help with the extra costs. A producer plans the show months ahead, designing the look of the show, then hiring companies to provide other elements such as the lighting, pyrotechnics, and stages. Beyoncé's stage at the 2013 performance in New Orleans was made of 35 pieces. The show used more than 1,000 light fixtures, which were set up by 600 volunteers.

IT'S ALL ABOUT AUDIENCE

Performing at the halftime show gives an artist exposure to about 110 million people. Even a famous band or performer will find new fans. The increased purchases and downloads of the performer's albums and songs immediately after the show proves that point.

Sponsors also pay to have their company name linked to the show for exposure to the show's audience. Companies, such as Oscar Mayer (meats), Bridgestone (tires), and AOL (Internet service provider), have been past sponsors. Pepsi is the latest show sponsor, paying an estimated $7 million for the right to call the show the Pepsi Super Bowl Halftime Show.

INSIDER INSIGHT

"Regardless of the performer's age or whether the songs are 'oldies but goodies' or new, a song featured during the Super Bowl halftime show can yield an exponential jump in sales, as music fans discover—or rediscover—an artist and their songs."
David Bakula, senior vice president of client insights at Nielsen

Beyoncé performed at the Super Bowl in New Orleans in 2013 during the Pepsi Halftime Show and saw a 40 percent boost to her own album sales and those of her former band, Destiny's Child.

In 2012, sales of the songs Madonna performed in the halftime show increased by 165 percent in the week after her performance. Before the show, her songs were purchased 197,000 times. But, afterward the number rose to 522,000.

HALFTIME PERFORMERS

Digital Track Purchases
Week After v. Week Before Super Bowl

Super Bowl	Super Bowl XLVI (2/5/12)	Super Bowl XLV (2/6/11)	Super Bowl XLIV (2/7/10)
Halftime Performer	Madonna (9 songs)	Black Eyed Peas (8 songs)	The Who (5 songs)
Total Purchases Week Before Super Bowl	197,000	196,000	12,000
Total Purchases Week After Super Bowl	522,000	406,000	59,000
% Increase in Purchases	165%	108%	396%

Halftime performers gain a huge rise in sales after their appearance.

OTHER BENEFITS

Does your local restaurant advertise specials for Super Bowl Sunday? Maybe you made a bet with a friend on the winning team? Super Bowl is such a big event that it creates many opportunities for other unrelated businesses to make money. Sometimes it means other businesses will lose money.

Yes! Ed Reed celebrates the Baltimore Ravens 2013 Super Bowl win in New Orleans. At the same time, many businesses all across the country celebrated the game's positive boost to their revenues.

SUPER BOWL FOOD CONSUMPTION
Food eaten over Superbowl weekend February 2013

1.23 billion chicken wings

4 million pizzas

50 million cases of beer

158 million avocados

Vast amounts of food and drink are consumed over Super Bowl weekend.

LOCAL EXTERNALITIES

If you watch Super Bowl at home, chances are you bought snack foods and things to drink from a local store. You just helped businesses in your neighborhood take advantage of Super Bowl externalities. In 2012, it was estimated that people in the United States spent $55 million on food and $237 million on drinks for the Super Bowl. How about betting? About $90 million in bets are placed for the Super Bowl, the biggest single-day-sports betting event of the year.

INTANGIBLE COSTS OR BENEFITS

What effect does a winning Super Bowl team have on the local economy? Some economists say it's only about a $180 annual increase per person. But a win may provide intangible benefits. City workers feel increased city pride through a winning team and may work harder. Happy people spend more money, giving a small boost to the local economy. After a win, more people attend home games the following year, where their spending increases the city's revenue, which in turn can benefit community-funded projects such as swimming pools and other resources for the community to enjoy.

Sometimes a win is a negative externality. During the 2013 parade through Baltimore, crowds were so huge that downtown businesses closed while others gave employees the day off. When businesses have to close, they can't make money. If employees can't get to work, the company still has to pay them. But there is an intangible benefit creating workers who are happy to celebrate at the parade.

WHAT DO YOU THINK?

The Super Bowl is expected to mean the sale of more than 1.25 billion chicken wings, the consumption of more than 150 million avocados, and more than 11 million pounds (5 million kilograms) of potato chips. Can you think of what types of businesses or industries might receive positive externalities from this?

Adam Vinatieri, a placekicker, has played in five Super Bowls. Signing autographs for fans is part of being a good representative for the team.

INSIDER INSIGHT
"If you are a great player on a losing team, the chances for national endorsements are slim. If you are a great player on a bad team in a small market, they are worse. Companies want winners!"
Jack Bechta, sports agent

TRICKS OF THE TRADE

Joe Flacco's contract with the Ravens was up but he stalled contract talks until the season was done. That move worked in his favor. After his Super Bowl win in 2013, where he was also awarded the game's Most Valuable Player, he signed a contract with Baltimore for $120.6 million over six years.

SALARY

What a win! A Super Bowl win brings many benefits. In 2012, the NFL paid winning team players $88,000 each and losing team players $44,000 each for being in the Super Bowl game. Winners also get a Super Bowl ring. NFL players sign contracts, which are binding agreements between a team and player that guarantee what the player will be paid. A player who performs well in the Super Bowl, such as a game MVP (most valuable player) is seen as more valuable and can ask for—and get—a much higher salary. There's no guarantee he'll perform that well again, but a team values players who perform well.

FAN FOLLOWING

A player who stands out in a Super Bowl becomes a familiar name to a mass audience, so he's likely to get a bigger fan following. The more fans a player has, the more likely he is to get an **endorsement** contract. That's when a well-known person promotes a product or service in an ad. But endorsement deals can be a risky investment for a company because, if the player suddenly becomes unpopular, it can reflect badly on the company.

A player with a lot of followers on social media can attract more fans to a game. More interaction with fans will increase interest in the player and the team he plays for, as well as in the NFL as a whole.

TRICKS OF THE TRADE

A team's highest paid players are usually quarterbacks. An NFL team has about three quarterbacks on a roster of 53 players. It's an important position. Fans recognize quarterbacks more easily since they have their helmet off more than other players when they talk to the media. Consumers recognize quarterbacks as representing a team's brand.

6 THE FUTURE OF THE SUPER BOWL

Will the trend toward ever-higher salaries, costs, ticket prices, revenues, and profits at the Super Bowl continue? How will the NFL continue to attract advertisers, fans, and more revenue? The NFL has big goals. It's looking into new markets and new ways to get the NFL's game in front of an even larger audience. It may even look at new types of business.

These San Francisco 49ers fans purchased team merchandise to show off their support for their favorite team.

Young fans wear Baltimore Ravens hats and jerseys to celebrate their team's Super Bowl win.

A BIG BILLION GOAL

In 2010, NFL commissioner Rodger Goodall stated that his goal for the league was to increase revenue to $25 billion by 2027. That figure represents a 163 percent increase over 17 years. How might that goal be reached? Sales of tickets and food for the game in the stadium itself may see only modest growth, as spending on these items can't exceed your budget to pay for them and stadiums are a fixed size. But new stadiums will be built and their more luxurious features sold at premium prices. New broadcast deals with different types of media will be negotiated. The NFL will look to see if it can expand into international markets to capture even more fans.

Today, you're keeping up with your favorite teams on many different devices such as laptops, mobile phones, and tablets. With these new devices, more markets are becoming available to the NFL. It will look for how to capture you as a fan on those different platforms. If companies that measure viewing habits can show that you do watch football on personal devices, then advertisers will be willing to pay more to get their messages to you. Once that happens, the NFL will charge more to carry their games.

OTHER AREAS

Will the NFL decide to expand the number of games played in the regular season or have more teams in the playoffs? It's been suggested that the NFL could get into sports gambling, or get into the apparel business themselves. No matter how they do it, it's clear that consumers like you will determine whether they make a profit.

HOW YOU SUPPORT SUPER BOWL

The cost of two adults visiting the Super Bowl event for the weekend.

Lodging: $400 x 3 nights = $1,200

Tickets: $2,500 x 2 people = $5,000

Flights: (At least) $1,400 x 2 people = $2,800

Parking: $300 for close–range spots

Car rental: $60 x 3 days = $180

Food: $100 x 3 days = $300

Game–day Snacks: $100

NFL Jersey: $100 x 2 = $200

Total $10,080

The cost of two adults going to the Super Bowl weekend can be more than $10,000.

EUROPEAN EXPANSION

Where is there a large population that hasn't been exposed to much professional football up to this point? The answer is Europe. That's where the NFL is looking to grow and expand. But there are some challenges. On the world sports market, American football faces competition from other more popular games in Europe such as soccer and rugby. In Europe, there is no grassroots base of young fans and high school and college football players like we have in North America.

But there are resources available. The NFL can take advantage of many existing soccer stadiums as well as stadiums constructed for past Olympic Games. The NFL has set up an office in London to generate broadcasting and licensing deals there. People with expertise in knowing how European consumers want to be entertained can help the NFL gain more market share. Specific European sponsorship deals, broadcast agreements, and promotional opportunities are all being planned.

THE CANADIAN FOOTBALL LEAGUE

The CFL is the professional football league in Canada. Nine teams currently make up the league. There are differences in the rules between the NFL and CFL games. Sometimes NFL players have moved to play in the smaller CFL market with great success.

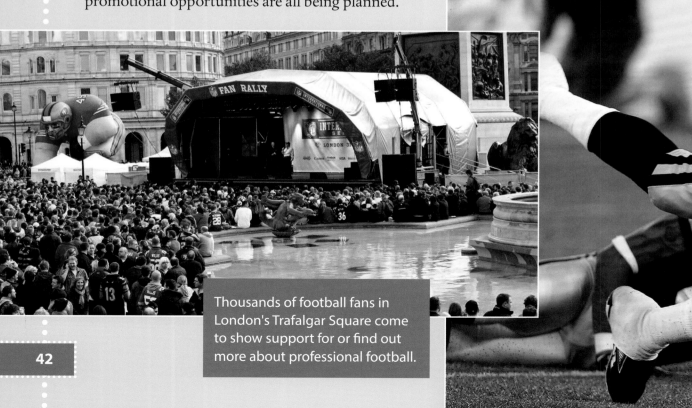

Thousands of football fans in London's Trafalgar Square come to show support for or find out more about professional football.

LOOKING TO LONDON

The International Series is a special annual NFL game that has been held since 2007. It started as a single game held in London but was expanded to two games in 2013, and there are plans to add a third in the near future. In this series, four NFL teams play in two regular season games at Wembley Stadium. Both 2013 games sold out weeks before they took place. It's a good sign that football might just find a strong market in Europe.

Do you think one day there will be NFL teams in European cities? One thing is for sure. As long as consumers like you keep watching and cheering on your favorite teams, there will be an NFL—and, of course, a Super Bowl.

GROWTH OF THE WORLDWIDE SPORTS ECONOMY

Global sports market by region (US$ Millions)

	Global revenues	% Change
2006	107,516	12.1
2007	111,934	4.1
2008	120,760	7.9
2009	112,489	-6.8
2010	121,391	7.9
2011	118,690	-2.2
2012	129,929	9.5
2013	130,164	0.2
2014	146,469	12.5
2015	145,341	-0.8

The global sports economy has grown fast since 2006. It is now predicted to slow.

The Canadian Football League teams kick off their season-opening game in their quest to make the final championship game, known as the Grey Cup.

GLOSSARY

aggregate demand The individual demand of everyone added together to form a total demand

assets Things owned that have value

bids Proposed plans for how to accomplish things, with prices attached for how to achieve the bids

brand A unique symbol, logo, words, or set of expectations that a company uses to set itself apart from other similar companies

budget A detailed plan that manages the money that is received (income) and the money that is spent or paid out (expense)

capitalism A system of economics in which trade and manufacturing are controlled by the people and businesses that are trying to make a profit

consumer A person who buys goods and services

contract Binding agreement between two organizations or people, for example between a team and a player

demand The amount of a resource consumers will buy

distributes Supplies goods and services to businesses to sell them

economics The study of how resources are distributed to satisfy wants and needs

endorsement A legal contract by which a person, such as a football player, promotes a product or service, often in an advertisement

expense The costs required to produce a good or service

externalities Unrelated businesses or organizations that are affected by an event such as the Super Bowl

fragments Breaks up a market into smaller parts

income The money that an individual receives in exchange for work or that a business receives for selling goods or services

indirect benefit Something that helps in a roundabout way

industry A group of businesses that are similar and that produce a similar product or service

intangible Something that does not have a physical form, so it can't be touched

invest To give money with the expectation that it will eventually create more money for the giver

GLOSSARY

lease A contract to use a property for a set period of time in exchange for regular set payments

license Formal permission to do something, often in exchange for a fee

macroeconomics A branch of economics that studies large economic factors that affect a country or countries, or a whole industry

market The exchange of goods or services

market economy An economic system in which consumers are free to choose what goods and services they spend their money on

mark-up An increase in the price

merchandise Commercial sales of products related to an industry or event

microeconomics A branch of economics that studies smaller economic factors such as the actions of individual consumers or businesses

monopoly Control of the supply or trade of something

oligopolistic Characteristics of a market that has only a few sellers

opportunity cost The cost of an action not taken

producer A company or individual who makes something to sell

profit The money left after all costs have been paid

receipt Money received

revenue streams The ways or forms of business in which a company makes money

salary Fixed payment made to an employee on a regular basis

sponsor To give money to a business or event as a way to advertise products or services

subsidiary A company controlled by another larger company

supply The amount of a resource available for selling

taxes A percentage of money added to the cost of goods or services that is given to a city, state, or national government

value-added Enhancements or extra benefits given to something to make it more attractive to buy

VIP A very important person

wages The money a worker earns for work or services; an income

FIND OUT MORE

BOOKS TO READ

Acton, Johnny, and David Goldblatt. *Eyewitness Books: Economy.* Dorling Kindersley, 2010.

Andrews, Carolyn. *What Are Goods and Services?* (Economics in Action). Crabtree Publishing, 2008.

Biskup, Agnieszka. *Football: How It Works* (Sports Illustrated Kids: The Science of Sports). Capstone Press, 2010.

Challen, Paul. *What Is Supply and Demand?* (Economics in Action). Crabtree Publishing, 2010.

Frederick, Shane. *Football: The Math of the Game* (Sports Illustrated Kids: Sports Math). Capstone Press, 2011.

Girard Golomb, Kristen. *Economics and You, Grades 5–8.* Mark Twain Media, 2012.

Gramling, Gary. *Sports Illustrated Kids 1st and 10: Top 10 Lists of Everything in Football.* Sports Illustrated Books, 2011.

Hollander, Barbara. *Money Matters: An Introduction to Economics.* Heinemann Raintree, 2010.

Hulick, Kathryn. *The Economics of a Video Game* (Economics of Entertainment). Crabtree Publishing, 2013.

Johnson, Robin. *The Economics of Making a Movie* (Economics of Entertainment). Crabtree Publishing, 2013.

Murray, Stuart A.P. *Score with Football Math* (Score with Sports Math). Enslow Elementary, 2013.

Perl, Sheri. *The Economics of a Rock Concert* (Economics of Entertainment). Crabtree Publishing, 2013.

WEBSITES

The National Football League
www.nfl.com

NFL kickoff
www.nfl.com/kickoff

Football history and trivia
www.footballgeography.com

NY/NJ Super Bowl
www.nynjsuperbowl.com

INDEX

REFERENCES

ACKNOWLEDGMENTS
Thanks to the following people for assistance and to these sources of information:

Websites:
The Bleacher Report: www.bleacherreport.com
Bloomberg: www.bloomberg.com
ESPN: www.espn.com
Forbes: www.forbes.com
Investopedia: www.investopedia.com
The Kearney Report: www.atkearney.com
National Football Post:
    www.nationalfootballpost.com
NFL: www.nfl.com
NFL London: www.nfllondon.net
Nielsen: www.nielsen.com
Plunkett Research, Ltd.:
    www.plunkettresearch.com
"Pro Football Talk" NBC Sports:
    http://profootballtalk.nbcsports.com
Sports Business Daily:
    www.sportsbusinessdaily.com
Statista: www.statista.com

Articles from newspapers & magazines:
"Beyoncé's Super Bowl Sales Impact: Final Chart Numbers," by Keith Caulfield, *Billboard*, February 13, 2013.
"Super Bowl Sunday: What We're Eating, Where We're Watching, How Much We're Spending," by Victor Luckerson, *Time, Business of Sports*, January 31, 2013.
"$14 for nachos and other insane Super Bowl concession prices," by Chris Chase, *USA Today*, February 3, 2013.
"MainGate Scores Huge Super Bowl Merchandising Deal," by Anthony Schoettle, *Indianapolis Business Journal*, July 23, 2013.
"How Much Business Does the Super Bowl Bring In?," by Dylan Kraslow, *Northwestern Business Review*, February 3, 2012.
"Parents to pull kids from school, businesses o close for parade," by Julie Scharper and Luke Broadwater, *The Baltimore Sun*, February 4, 2013.
"Nice Super Bowl parade for the Ravens; now Baltimore says show me the money," by David Hill, *The Washington Times*, February 14, 2013.
"How Much Do Players Get Paid for Winning the Super Bowl?" by Darren Rovell, CNBC, January 18, 2011.
"Super Bowl 50 Will Be in Smartest Stadium in NFL," by Martha Mendoza, *Associated Press*, May 28, 2013.
"Super Bowl bidding process challenges creativity," by Bill Baker, *The Times-Picayune*, May 18, 2009.
"What Happens to the Losing Team's Championship Shirts?," by Matt Soniak, *Mental Floss*, February 2, 2013.
"Being an NFL Cheerleader—The Fans, the Pay, the Workouts," by Steve Mazzucchi, *Lemondrop*, February 16, 2010.
"EXCLUSIVE: Beyoncé will PAY 'hundreds of thousands' of dollars to sing at the Super Bowl (but don't worry – she'll make millions from it anyway)," by Sara Nathan, The *Daily Mail*, January 28, 2013.

Reports:
"Padding Required: Assessing the Economic Impact of the Super Bowl," Victor A. Matheson and Robert A. Baade, September 2004.
"The Intangible Benefits of Sports Teams," Jeffrey G. Owen, *Public Finance and Management*, Volume Six, Number 3, pp. 321–345, 2006.
"The Economic Impact of Super Bowl XLVI: Accounting the Full Economic Benefits to the Indianapolis Metropolitan Area," Rockport Analytics, July 2012.

Two-Minute Animal Stories

Six Stories Featuring Frisky, Funny Animals

Written and illustrated
by AMYE ROSENBERG

A GOLDEN BOOK • NEW YORK
Western Publishing Company, Inc., Racine, Wisconsin 53404

The Pie Snatcher

Bratty Raccoon didn't like to work. He preferred to poke around the treetops, looking for trouble.

Bratty Raccoon was always hungry. One morning the smell of something delicious wafted to his treetop. He followed his nose, and he soon came to a cottage. A sign over the door said, "Hedgehog's Pie Shop—Serving the Forest for Forty Years."

"I think I'll sample a pie," thought Bratty Raccoon.

Just then Mr. and Mrs. Hedgehog came out of the shop with Old Mother Rabbit. Old Mother Rabbit carried a pie in her basket.

Bratty Raccoon stepped boldly up to Old Mother Rabbit. "Good day!" he said cheerfully. "May I carry your basket for you?"

"How nice of you," replied Old Mother Rabbit. But, as she held out her basket, Bratty Raccoon reached in, snatched the pie, and fled.

Mr. Hedgehog, who had seen it all, tried to catch the rascal. But Bratty Raccoon shot up a tree, clutching his prize.

The old Hedgehogs stood helpless. Old Mother Rabbit returned home with an empty basket.

The next day Bratty Raccoon waited on the stone wall outside the pie shop. Brown Bear had just purchased a gooseberry pie, which he was balancing on his head. Bratty snatched the pie and ran away.

Early the next morning Old Mother Rabbit and Brown Bear returned to the pie shop. The Hedgehogs had a plan to catch Bratty. Mrs. Hedgehog handed everyone a brush and a bucket of fresh creamy butter.

Old Mother Rabbit painted the stone wall with butter. Mr. Hedgehog coated the tree branches. Brown Bear stood on a ladder and splashed the roof.

Then Mrs. Hedgehog set a cherry pie to cool on the windowsill. They all hid in the bushes and waited.

Bratty Raccoon soon appeared. He spotted the cherry pie, snatched it, and strolled down the path. Suddenly Mr. and Mrs. Hedgehog popped up from behind the bushes. So did Old Mother Rabbit and Brown Bear.

Startled, Bratty Raccoon sprang for the nearest tree branch, but the buttered branch slipped out of his grasp. He tried to climb the stone wall, but his feet slipped on the buttered stones. Then Bratty scrambled up the chimney.

As he leapt out onto the roof to make his escape, his feet flew out from under him. Bratty Raccoon plopped to the ground in a sticky heap.

The pie snatcher was caught!

Now the pie shop is busier than ever—and so is Bratty Raccoon. Oh, he'd still prefer to poke around treetops, looking for trouble, but it is not likely he will ever find the time.

Albert's New Suit

It was the day of the Porklys' garden party. Albert's whole family was invited.

Mama dressed Albert in the new suit she had made for him. She said, "Run along until the rest of the family is ready. Don't eat anything—it will spoil your appetite. And don't get dirty."

Albert went out to the garden. The Porklys lived next door, so Albert could hear them preparing, but he could not see over the hedge between their gardens. He climbed the pear tree, and there he had a fine view of the goings-on.

Mr. Porkly was blowing up balloons. Mrs. Porkly was decorating a gigantic chocolate cake. The little Porklys were carrying out sandwiches, puddings, and pies.

Albert got very hungry. He plucked a pear from a nearby branch and bit into it. The juice ran down his chin onto his new jacket. "I'd better clean this before Mama sees it," thought Albert. He began to climb down. Suddenly a branch caught the seat of Albert's new pants. When he reached behind to feel the damage, the branch he was standing on broke. Albert fell into the dirt below.

He got up and looked at his torn and soiled new suit. "I'd better fix this before Mama sees it," thought Albert. He sneaked into the house and tiptoed upstairs.

Albert went into Mama and Papa's room to look at himself in the mirror. He spotted his parents' clothes on the bed. Mama's sewing basket was nearby. That gave Albert an idea.

He snipped a piece from Papa's vest. "He won't miss this," thought Albert. He sewed the piece to the seat of his pants. Then he cut two tiny squares from Mama's skirt and sewed them onto the knees of his pants.

Albert heard someone coming and sneaked into his sister's room. He saw her bonnet. He snipped a little from here and there. Then he sewed the pieces to the soiled elbows of his jacket.

Once again Albert heard someone coming. He ran into Grandma's room, where he spotted her shawl.

Albert cut off a piece of the shawl and wrapped it around his neck. It covered the stain on the front of his jacket.

Albert strolled into the bathroom to admire himself in the mirror.

Just then he heard a bellow down the hall. "There's a hole in my vest!"

"There are two holes in my skirt!"

"My bonnet's been bitten!"

"My shawl is ruined!"

Then, "A-A-A-Albert!" The family burst into the bathroom. One look at Albert explained everything.

"There's my skirt!" cried Mama, pointing at Albert's knees.

"There's my bonnet!" cried Albert's sister, pointing at his elbows.

"There's my shawl!" cried Grandma, pointing at the front of Albert's jacket.

"Where's my vest, then?" Papa demanded angrily.

Albert turned around to show the seat of his pants. When he saw the look in Papa's eyes, Albert bolted out the window into the branches of the pear tree.

"You can stay there till dark!" Mama cried.

"You can watch us having a good time!" thundered Papa.

And that's just what Albert did.

Maisie's Mean Trick

One day Maisie Mouse and Pip Chipmunk went walking by the seaside. "Tell me," said Maisie Mouse, "the thing you do best."

Pip replied, "I'm a strong swimmer. That's what I do best of all."

"That's not important," said Maisie. "I'm a great builder. I can build a sand castle that is so strong, no one can break it. Would you like me to show you?"

Pip said he would. He flopped down on the sand to watch.

"I have an idea," Maisie said. "I'll cover you with sand and build the castle on top of you!"

"That sounds like fun!" said Pip. He lay very still while Maisie buried him up to his whiskers. She packed the sand firmly.

Then she shaped the towers and tunnels. "There!" declared Maisie. "Now try to break my sand castle!"

Pip wriggled, struggled, and sweated. But he could not break free of the sand castle.

"Whew!" he puffed. "You were right. This is too strong to break. You'll have to dig me out."

Maisie just laughed. "Get yourself out! And if a big wave comes up and gets you first, then you can show what a great swimmer you are!"

She scampered away, laughing at poor Pip and her own clever trick. She laughed so hard that she did not notice the waves rising behind her. Suddenly a gigantic wave struck Maisie.

She tumbled into the water and was swept far out to sea. "Help, Pip!" Maisie shrieked. "I can't swim!"

But it was no use. Pip could not free himself to save her, though he tried and tried. The waves rolled over little Maisie. Slowly she sank toward the bottom of the sea.

A big fish saw her struggling. "This is your lucky day, land creature," gurgled the fish. "Grab hold of my tail!"

The fish swam toward the shore, pulling Maisie behind.

As they neared the shore Pip caught sight of Maisie clinging to the big fish's tail. "Oh, no!" Pip gasped. "Maisie will be swallowed by a giant sea creature!"

Pip struggled harder than ever. With a surge of strength, he broke the sand castle and leapt to his feet.

He was just in time. The fish flicked its tail and tossed Maisie high over the shore. She landed in Pip's outstretched arms.

"Please forgive me!" Maisie wailed. "My meanness nearly got me drowned! I'll never trick you again—I promise!"

Pip said, "Promise me you will learn how to swim. It could save your life!"

So Maisie Mouse learned how to swim. She learned never to play mean tricks. And she learned that the best thing of all is to be a good friend.

Tad the Baddie

Oh, Tad the baddie was a bully, even for a mouse.

He tied his sisters' tails in knots and dragged them round the house.

"I'm bigger, stronger!" Tad would boast. "I'm better than you all!"

He pinched his sisters on the ears and bounced them off the wall.

The sisters knew a friendly cat. They sought his wise advice.

The cat was big and scary, but was always nice to mice.

"Our bully brother pinches, he pulls our tails and ears!

He hits and bites and scratches—and knocks us on our rears!

We only want to scare him—not hurt him, no, indeed.

Please help teach him a lesson." So the friendly cat agreed.

Next day Tad the baddie was the meanest little mouse.

He sprayed his sisters with the hose and broke their ginger house.

The sisters, who'd had quite enough, now warned their brother, Tad,

"The Mouse-eater will get you, if you keep on being bad!"

But Tad kept up his naughty tricks, not thinking of the beast,

When the cat sprang up behind the wall and cried, "A lunchtime feast!"

"Oh, please, take Tad," the sisters said, "for we are only small.

Tad's stronger and much bigger—he'll be the tastiest of all!"

Tad cried, "Don't eat me, Mr. Cat—
I'm sorry that I boasted!
I'm just a silly, scrawny mouse—
and not too tasty roasted!
I'll be nicer to my sisters now—
I'll put away their toys,
I'll shine their shoes and make their beds—
I'll be the best of boys!"

Tad's kinder to his sisters now,
And the cat comes round to tea.
Tad bakes the cakes and pours the cream,
And he's good as he can be!

The Scary Bell Tower

One morning three little squirrels named Sam, Simon, and Nell came out of their home in an oak tree. They were going out to explore the world for the first time.

"Have fun," said their mother. "And remember to stay away from the village and the people there."

"What are people?" asked little Nell.

"They are very large," explained Mother. "They do not have fur or bushy tails. They are noisy. And they live in big homes made of stones."

The squirrels thought people sounded scary. "We will be careful," they promised, and they set out to discover new things.

Nell discovered that berries were fun to toss like balls. She tossed a big red berry to Simon. Simon tossed it back. But the berry fell behind a hedge. "Let's go fetch it!" Nell squealed.

On the other side of the hedge, the little squirrels saw something strange. It was a tall heap of stones. At the top some shiny things glistened in the sun.

"This looks like one of those people homes Mother warned us about," whispered Sam.

"We'd better turn back," said Simon.

"Don't be such babies," insisted Nell. "We will never learn anything about the world if we don't have a good look. Come on!"

The little squirrels climbed up the stones until they were as high as the treetops. They looked up at the large smooth, shiny objects above them and the ropes that hung down.

"These look like fun to swing on," said Simon. "And it is cool and shady in here."

The three little squirrels each grabbed a rope. They swung gently at first. It was very pleasant.

"I want to swing higher!" said Sam.

"I want to swing harder!" said Simon.

"I want to swing faster!" said Nell.

So they swung higher and harder and faster in the bell tower. But, as they swung, they heard a strange noise. *Cling, clang!*

Then a louder *bing, bang!*

Then an even louder *ding, dong!*

"What could it be?" thought each little squirrel.

"These shiny things are very large," thought each at the same time.

"They don't have fur or bushy tails," thought each at the same time.

"They are noisy," thought each at the same time.

"And they live in a big home made of stones," thought each at the same time.

Then all three squirrels cried out at the same time, "Yikes! People!"

They slid down the ropes as fast as they could and squeezed under a door.

They ran and ran until they
reached their home in the oak tree.
They rushed to their mother and told
her what had happened.

Their mother explained the difference between bells and
people. "I hope you learned something today," she said.
    "I learned," said Sam, "that there is always
something new to learn in the world."
    "I learned," said Simon, "that there
are both wonderful and frightening
things in the world."
    "And I learned," said little Nell,
"that when I'm frightened, I have a
safe home and a wise mother to make
me feel better."

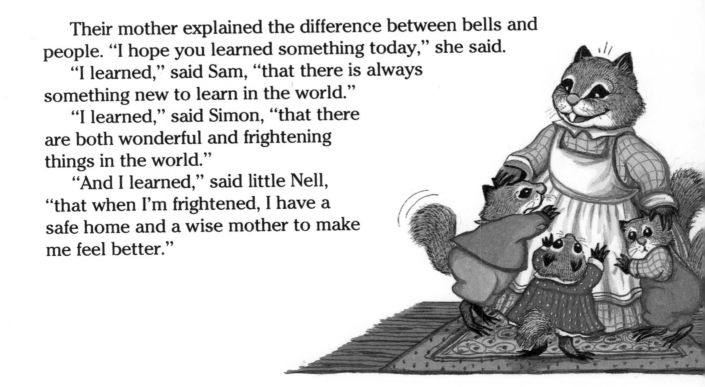

Good Night, Sailor Mice

Once six little mice built a boat. They had to pretend to sail it, because real rivers and streams are far too dangerous for little mice.

It happened to rain one summer night. The little mice knew that the big puddles left by the rain were safe to sail on. And they knew the sun would dry up the puddles by morning.

So, instead of going straight to bed that night, the mice sneaked out to sail their boat on the biggest puddle they could find.

"How will we know where to sail?" asked one mouse.

Another mouse replied, "We will sail until we see the moon in the water. Then we must go straight home to bed before anyone discovers we're gone."

The six little ones did just that. And on their way home to their snug little beds, they sang this song:

> "We built a wee houseboat (we call it a mouseboat)—
> We are six merry mice on the river,
> With a cork for a float and a sail from a coat
> And the moon grinning down, just a sliver."

Good night!